Praise for Fiston Mwanza Mujila

"After all the riches that have been torn from his country by foreigners, asks this remarkable poet, 'will they also find a way to haul away the Congo River and use it as room freshener?' Mwanza Mujila's raw and passionate work is an authentic voice from a long-suffering land whose story we are too often accustomed to hearing only from outsiders."

—Adam Hochschild, author of *King Leopold's Ghost: A Story of Greed, Terror, and Heroism in Colonial Africa*

"The beauty of Mwanza Mujila's poetry comes from the telescoping of pain and despair into a language of unexpected juxtapositions. The resemblance with Dambudzo Marechera is not accidental, for they both attempt to hurl language into the abyss and to decipher the vague and mangled echoes that return to them in that act. A new and provocative contribution to African Literature." —Ato Quayson, Stanford University

"The poems show the Congo River running through Mwanza Mujila's veins as he contemplates mortality, (in)voluntary exile, the resource curse and the physical grandeur of the river itself. . . . These translations are a must-read." —Efemia Chela, *Johannesburg Review of Books*

"Translation is the ultimate tribute, a tributary to the river of beauty and this is so present in *The River in the Belly*. This is an urgent book that will outlive us all, but we can excavate it now. There is anguish. But for each wound Mwanza Mujila opens and tenderly kneads, he also sutures with a deep love. We must listen!"

—Mukoma Wa Ngugi, author of *Logotherapy* and *Black Star Nairobi*

"This book . . . is a masterpiece of poetic imagination and excellence. It is a melancholic meditation on the Congo River and the huge country named after it, while also expressing from the poet's new home in Austria his homesickness, solitude, and nostalgia for the good things he remembers from his country of origin." —Georges Nzongola-Ntalaja, author of *The Congo from Leopold to Kabila: A People's History*

"A book urgently wondering about deprivation, desire, violence, animal– human relations, exile, music, madı̈ ⁣ ⁣ ⁣ ⁣ ⁣ lese urbanities. Exquisite and profounc

—Nancy ⁣ ⁣ ⁣ ⁣ ⁣ ⁣ tate: *Violence,* ⁣ ⁣ ⁣ ⁣ ⁣ ⁣ ongo

"Fiston Mwanza Mujila . . . thinks back not only to his native river, but also to the almost constant multi-agent civil war that has eviscerated the Congo over the past decades: it is both the bloodiest conflict of our time and one of the least noticed. . . . Maney very capably conveys the intonations and registers of the original in this faithful and beautiful rendering."

—Eugene Ostashevsky, judge for the 2019 *Asymptote*
Close Approximations International Translation Contest

"A travelogue featuring dyspeptic saints, sophic beasts and, above all, an all-consuming river. Wonderfully subversive."

—Jason Stearns, author of *Dancing in the Glory of Monsters:*
The Collapse of the Congo and the Great War of Africa

The River in the Belly

Fiston Mwanza Mujila

PHONEME
MEDIA

DEEP
VELLUM

DALLAS, TEXAS

Phoneme Media, an imprint of Deep Vellum
3000 Commerce St., Dallas, Texas 75226
deepvellum.org · @deepvellum

Deep Vellum is a 501c3 nonprofit literary arts organization
founded in 2013 with the mission to bring
the world into conversation through literature.

Support for this publication has been provided in part by a grant from the City
of Dallas Office of Arts and Culture's ArtsActivate program and Amazon Literary
Partnership.

ISBNs: 978-1-64605-067-3 (paperback) | 978-1-64605-068-0 (ebook)

LIBRARY OF CONGRESS: 2021936717

Front cover by Justin Childress | justinchildress.co

Interior Layout and Typesetting by KGT

Printed in the United States of America

In memory of Mwanza Mujila Pierre (1948–2021)

SOLITUDE 61

a river convulses in my belly
a confounded malingerer, dirty and immense, mournful and
    malign,
a river in the late stages of dysentery . . .

SOLITUDE 71

a restless, twitchy dog (?)
the river mopes as the day lengthens
it snivels without knowing just why
it's been sniveling since Babel, since old Noah and his flood
since the prophet Ezekiel, since sister Abigail . . .
its trail of snot stretching across an absurd span . . .

SOLITUDE 52

a restless, twitchy dog (?)
and the farce that thaws
between two frozen smiles
I sell my flesh to the firstcomer
in the depths of this sky uncorking its slobber
anyhow, I'm off to bark with the dogs
at the peak of the second solar eclipse in Katako-Kombe

SOLITUDE 73

a restless, twitchy dog (?)
and I lay claim to my leprosy
and I lay claim to my right to vomit
and I lay claim to my Russian roots
and I lay claim to the juices of the body
of my dismembered body
as it was in the beginning . . .

SOLITUDE 38

Christ won't be shouted down twice in a row
those who plan to make it their business
will have to bide their time
long enough for their teeth and pubes to fall out
long enough for their jizz and desire
to burn the Book of Genesis and the First Epistle
of Paul to the Corinthians to fade

SOLITUDE 3

the river's nostalgia
is in not knowing where to stash its pox
not knowing what to do with its falls
it is the story of the baker who dies of hunger
the story of the cobbler who goes unshod . . .

SOLITUDE 64 *or nausea is prior to essence*

I have been pregnant for seventeen years, thirty-six months, and
two days. I make love to the sky. I'm expecting a child with the
sky. The child who comes out of my belly or the river born from
my loins or the river-child my misbegotten body spits out will fill
long nights of insomnia with its flesh . . . The child will go by the
name of Nzete ya mbila bazokata ezokola. Then will I be able to
boast (to any who will listen) of being mother and father to this
blurred creature, to this centipede creature, to this flat-tire crea-
ture—so needlessly grotesque.

SOLITUDE 57 *oder die Poesie der Verzweiflung or the cries of an empty body*

. . . I search for the remains of my body strewn across beaches of despair, left leg a figment, belly and groin as if punched from a press, hands stinking of goods and my yelps reaching not even to the ankles of this unelectrified sky, which is to say, I cheat the life holding me fast by the jaws, which is to say, I serve as decor to my future in a knotted garbage bag, to my amphibi-an-future, my kipelekese-future, my tchanga madesu-future . . .

. . . perhaps I must (in the hope of some sort of salvation) groan and bleat in D minor like my grandmother's last goat: beh, beh, beh . . .

. . . and to think there's no euthanasia for the stubborn and the drunkards of my kind! and to think there won't be a sec-ond, successive flood to sweep me away in my slobber, which is another way of saying that old Noah won't show his face around here again, won't march into the ark the seven pairs of all clean beasts—the male and the female—which is another way of saying the waters of the Zaire River, ebale ezanga mokuwa, will no longer lap at our desires for luxury and dec-adence beneath the starry nights of red-light districts in Kinshasa and Amsterdam . . .

. . . and meanwhile, without gods or even a loyal pet at my side, deprived of the salt of life, my centipede body crawls across beaches of despair, behind me, a dozen of my own teeth yanked out by vengeful shades and other scavengers of this unfired sky . . .

. . . all that's left is to bleat like Tshela, my grandmother Julienne mua Mwanza's last goat, like the mezzo-soprano Tshela: beh, beh, beh . . .

SOLITUDE 67

I am up to my neck in sun
and it is not from solitude
just my desire to scoff at the sea
the same sea that swept out with its bric-a-brac
my tinkerer's shop of dreams

SOLITUDE 25

two murders in two days
five murders in six days
six murders in five days
eight murders in eight days

SOLITUDE 41

I'm not the first to leave the continent
my exile won't be the exile of a race
even if I die today in Minsk
or in early afternoon in Vladivostok
no city will fall quiet, no nation will mourn
I see only my mother crumple—her eyes tear up
a few friends get knots in their stomachs
the Congo River will run its nightly course
in Uele and Bas-Zaïre
the copper factories will hum in Katanga
the grown-up and child soldiers aching for sex
drunk on blood and head will shepherd their
flocks between Buta and Isiro
and the freight trains will depart from Musumba to Ngandajika
passing through Ilebo, Kasangulu, Lwambo, Lodja and Kamituga

SOLITUDE 2

To my knowledge, to my sole knowledge, the sun rises in Lisala and sets in Tshela or Tsiela-Mbanga or better yet Tsiela, no offense to the brooders who still deny the solar eclipse in Katako-Kombe . . .
End of paragraph.

I long to see with my own eyes Mbuji Mayi wa balengela, Mbuji-Mayi for short, formerly Bakwanga, hometown of my great-grandfather, right on the Mbuji-Mayi river (meaning "goat-water" or "water-goat," depending who you ask), known for its anarchic sprawl, its ever growing population, its salivating, and its diamonds that rain down on you from the heavens . . .
End of paragraph.

I long to reunite with Tshimbalanga, the second youngest of my uncles, lost for all time in the diamond mines somewhere between Dimbelenge and Tshikapa . . .
End of paragraph.

I long for Kinshasa in a lull, or Lubumbashi, my country's left leg sunk in Northern Rhodesia, otherwise known as Zambia . . .
End of paragraph.

My disquiet is sluggish and long and agonizing and lustful like the railway line connecting Bumba, Aketi, Isiro, and Mungbere . . . Only the migrating birds can replenish their dreams and defeat asepsis,

which means the sun's rage is only equaled by the retching in
Noah's wake . . .
End of paragraph.

SOLITUDE 11

asleep but not
my sun running on fumes
my skeleton unboned
and my teeth serrated
(like cassava leaves)
must I shame my own flesh
or graze my own pubes?

SOLITUDE 96

leading a frog's life
is easier for me

SOLITUDE 17

and yes, amen! my poetic word
is not the Gospel of John
nor the First Epistle of Paul to the Corinthians
not even the Book of Habakkuk
which is my way of telling you
I water my dreams with sleep
since my sterile, desiccated bones
derail the train to the abyss

SOLITUDE 21

and yes, but no, my australopithecine gullet
and yes, but neither, my protozoan mug
and yes, but no, my skeletal body
and yes, but neither, my amphibian belly
am I a toad?
the toaderino (?)

SOLITUDE 32

I sleep with my shoes on

SOLITUDE 53

I refuse with my blood
I refuse with my cock
I refuse with my voice
I refuse with my teeth
brand my back with your soldering iron
from my rotting mouth
no syllable shall sound

SOLITUDE 9

I've got a fire in my belly
I feel the flames
flash up my throat
and out my nose
mouth, eyes, ears
am I in Gehenna?
is this burning flesh
my own?

SOLITUDE 79

(for dismembered bodies, saxophone solo, and piano-bar vibe;
the scene: Club Cuba/Club Ethiopia/Bar B-52, on the far left, the
girls from La Seleçao, behind them, the waitresses and busgirls,
front and center, the uninspired musicians suffering from syph-
ilis and even snail fever, shabby, grumpy and unwashed, on all
sides, the clubgoers standing, seated, squatting on the asphalt,
glued to the walls, pinned to the rafters and windowsills, drinking
straight from the bottle, showering each other with insults, mas-
turbating left-handed, dancing the horse dance, and singing the
chorus of our uninspired musicians suffering from syphilis and
even snail fever, shabby, grumpy and unwashed, under the rav-
enous gaze of the waitresses and busgirls demanding their tips at
the top of their lungs (like Panurgian sheep), threatening us with
curses and incurable diseases if we insist on acting like Tintin, lost
in Zimbabwe, such as, for example, the zibouille: you're walking
down the middle of the street when you lose control, strip off your
clothes, and take off at a gallop; the tsoumbie: you have to piss and
once you start, you can't stop, as if you had the whole Congo River
in your bladder; the gniognio: you eat and eat but never feel full;
the soupele, or nkirindanda, that the busgirl with the full lips cast
on one of our buddies, in which you vomit for two days and two
nights straight)

~~~~~~

I don't worship scabrous gods

stagehand and peanut-selling gods: days spent

smuggling guns and selling genitals: nights

they won't see me in their temple

on bended knee or lapping up some eucharist

fortified with blood, or dancing the polka or murmuring

elephantine prayers or wrecking my pipes singing kwashiorkor

     hymns to lighten their frog-like afternoons!

I am not their zoo (to be paraded out as lunch for their circus-

     cravings)

what I'm saying is that I am not their zoo!

and Tshimbalanga, the second youngest of my uncles

isn't here to make me measure my words!

scram, scram, scram! I bare my teeth

not a gum more, not a canine less

so be it . . . we'll invent a new land

on the very spot their chicken coop once stood

so be it . . . we'll order the stars to put a lid on their saucepans and

     suitcases

and climb aboard the first train for Kasangulu

so be it . . . we'll move mountains and seas

and if they raise the resistenza, these scabrous gods!

we'll let loose the four-headed hounds, and with the flood

they cadge from old Noah

for old Noah knows something about floods!

rain spattering like diarrhea will fill

your mouth, your ears, your nostrils, your teeth, your toes, your

knees, your chins, your bellies, and everything else!

I am not their zoo!

I don't worship scabrous gods

bapumbafu, souanpantes, bambendre

sadomasochists and Papuan soothsayers

SOLITUDE 66

my death won't be the extinction of a lineage
end of story!

SOLITUDE 45

a body so refined and warm
like day's end on one of our African savannas
how not to sink into revery or stupor or wordlessness or delirium
tremens and see the world in grenadine red?

SOLITUDE 40

shine, sun, for our bodies-in-blood
our bodies dismembered and our bodies made gaunt
shine, sun, for our souls made hard
our wastepaper souls, our souls rotten to the core
because it seems we are
the exegete of a bone-tired civilization
and want only your warm rays
to invent a second nature
a life-in-cardboard, a life on standby, a life
of a shorn sheep, all the same a life, no matter the
ingredients that outlast our bodies lost in ecstasy
over hopes befitting a buzzard or toad!

SOLITUDE 12

I don't live in exile
exile lives in me
I sling the world
over my shoulder
my left hand
reaches Malaysia
and my side
brushes Belarus
ravenous bulk-body
deprived of the good Lord and birdsong
I am myself exile
myself nausea
myself anxiety
myself askew . . .

SOLITUDE 63

I chow down on my shirt and underthings
I watch you gnash your teeth in shame and even hate
wish me a hearty meal
instead of cutting me down
to egg you on to murder, my own
I recount the history of my grub
I chow down on my trousers
I chow down on my ties
I chow down on my socks
I chow down on my underwear

SOLITUDE 85

I swallow my spit

SOLITUDE 36

the sky comes up to my knees
and the night (with its dicey looks)
boycotts my slumber
which is to say I cross through the night
with the help of bottles of shady home brew
and other spirits made in makeshift stills
which is to say I suffer from myopia
so extreme I must squint through a fog
to glimpse tomorrow's bleatings
and also from some sort of presbyopia
bad enough to mix up the colors
of my underwear
which amounts to saying all I've got are teeth
to graze on my own flesh
should I go ahead and wish myself good eating
or rattle off a requiem for my baffled
body?

SOLITUDE 13

we've seen prophets caught red-handed smoking grass . . .

we've seen prophets ministering at the bedside of a smalltime, snot-
nosed dictator, a backward despot spewing diarrhea . . .

we've seen prophets praying over weapons destined to blow a
school for disabled kids to bits . . .

we've seen prophets mingling in a haze of cigarettes, blowjobs, red
wine, masturbation, masked balls . . .

we've seen prophets outmode the Book of Habakkuk and the First
Epistle of Paul to the Corinthians . . .

prophecies on prophecies on prophecies on prophecies on prophe-
cies on prophecies on prophecies

and on top of all that . . .

to them, God is nothing more than a flyleaf

and on top of all that . . .

to them, God is nothing more than the back cover of a book

and even then . . .

their feet stink of unspeakable filth

SOLITUDE 34

the sun is chapped and dirty and woozy and rotten, it has the look
of someone who hasn't eaten in two days, the look of a child that
refuses to go to church because of rumors of sorcerer-crocodiles . . .

SOLITUDE 29

our mothers said that madness begins when you start to climb the chairs and the walls and the tree, perhaps I've already begun my madness and tomorrow I'll cross the street, bare-chested, on an empty stomach, lips quivering, teeth clacking at the sky . . .

SOLITUDE 4

a few glasses of red wine is all it takes

well, a good beer, too, to find myself on the streets where I was
born . . .

sometimes even in peculiar cities like New Jersey and Kathmandu
and Beirut and Singapore and Tokyo and Bethlehem and
Istanbul and Harlem and Khartoum and Mogadishu and
Antananarivo and Beijing and Nairobi and Sarajevo and
Cologne and Paris and Liège and . . .

have you already set foot in Kathmandu? what about Inhambane,
or as they say in Portuguese, Província de Inhambane,

this province of Mozambique that stares the Indian Ocean right
smack in the nose?

I sometimes stretch my legs in Inhambane and once spent an
entire year there, in 1763, a date marking the construction of
a fort, the Forte de Nossa Senhora da Conceição, that allowed
Inhambane, formerly bush and brush, to rise to the status of a
city like Kinshasa, formerly Léopoldville, daughter of the light
notwithstanding her eternal nights of rolling blackouts and
other debaucheries, or Graz with its Schlossberg and its con-
certs—jazz, jazz, jazz, and free jazz!

SOLITUDE 19

In the name of some kind of peace, after seizing both Kivus, after taking our diamonds, copper, cobalt, coltan, and uranium, after torching our fields, after trashing our schools and hospitals, after cutting our electricity, after raping our grandmothers and reducing our mothers to sexual slaves, after castrating our fathers and condemning our uncles to forced labor, after sabotaging the Inga Dam, after desecrating our cemeteries and keeping us from mourning our dead, will they also find a way to haul away the Congo River and use it as room freshener? This is not a question. It may or may not be an open secret: the river will drown anyone who so much as touches a hair on its head . . .

SOLITUDE 86

The Congo has no reason to envy other rivers.

It's got their froth, their hard-on, and the virulence to scare you
stiff. At the end of the day, it doesn't even need to take the family
deduction or apply for a visa to be a river. It was a river.

It is a river. It will remain a river. A river without nationality.
A free river. An independent river. An uppercase river.
A RIVER–RIVER!

SOLITUDE 47

not blood but the Congo River

sloshes in my veins . . .

if you deny it, if you have your doubts, if you don't believe me,
   pick up a sharp object (a steak knife or bayonet will do) and cut
   me open, slice me up, skin me from belly to belly, from head to
   toe . . .

you'll see what you see . . .

the left leg of the river . . .

where my guts should be

didn't they tell you my mouth stinks of Lake Munkamba, once
   infested with schistosomiasis?

didn't they tell you the Nyiragongo beats in lieu of my heart?

didn't they tell you my hair is the equatorial rain forest?

didn't they tell you my tears are lava from Nyamulagira and my
   laughter is the gusts that blow on Mwene-Ditu and Kanyama
   Kasese?

SOLITUDE 46

in spite of these tornadoes
that flatten us overnight
in spite of these swine fevers
and endless columns of diarrhea
in spite of these wishes to burn it down
to flip off bad luck, to spread the plague
the same poetry remains, the same spark, the same dew
paving with bituminous light our madcap dusks, our depraved
faces, our unleashed-dog destinies . . .
in the Third World
Jakarta and Kinshasa share a room
take the hallway on the left, toward the elevators
and since we are there
I say to your city, your words are husked by these winds that
    nightly stride the Sahara and the Argentine pampas . . .

SOLITUDE 6

For the power of the horses is in their mouths and in their tails; their tails are like serpents, with heads, and by means of them they wound.

The rest of mankind, who were not killed by these plagues, did not repent of the works of their hands nor give up worshiping demons and idols of gold and silver and bronze and stone and wood, which cannot either see or hear or walk; nor did they repent of their murders or their sorceries or their immorality or their thefts.

(Revelation 9:19–21, RSV)

SOLITUDE 43

to each their own way of grazing on life
my own, I refuse to sip daintily from a spoon
I gnaw, chew, suck, and smoke it
until it becomes feces and dust
between my uncircumcised cannibal jaws!

SOLITUDE 84

beyond any shadow of a doubt . . .
I'll invent a spare body, a thimble
to warehouse my nausea, as sopping
wet as the rains in Noah's wake

SOLITUDE 39

the sky weeps crocodile tears

it cries, it weeps, it cries, and it stops . . .

it cries, it weeps, it cries, and it stops . . .

it cries, it weeps, it cries, and it stops . . .

the rain . . .

a sheen of poetry to beat back

the burning sun

of these last days

this old-fart sun . . .

this cow-dung sun . . .

this cunning sun . . .

this wheelbarrow sun . . .

hallelujah, hallelujah, hallelujah

give Yahweh the glory due his name . . .

Deuteronomy 11:14

SOLITUDE 8

my leprosy gives birth to a white mouse! in the agony of the
trombone my nausea exults! in the agony of the trombone is a song
of despair! in the agony of the trombone is a song of farewell! and
utopia infected with smallpox shits to the point of exhaustion!
and recites a litany of schlock in a magnificent decrescendo! and
the river narrows and prefigures its suicide in the ocean thirsting
for seed! redemption no. 1: the driving rain is slobber spit up
by a babbling god! redemption no. 2: the slobber expectorates
our bodies-in-blood! redemption no. 3: early deliverance as
Christ negotiates with God the Father for our final rapture and
involuntary purification bibukuta-bukuta, bangubu lokoso,
basemba-bilokota!

SOLITUDE 81

Father used to ask me why I looked like I was marching when I danced. When I told him dancing made my stomach hurt, he took me to the doctor not once, but twice. Even then, I couldn't bring myself to tell him I'd learned to dance in an army camp.

Everybody knew father. I couldn't smoke a cigarette, skip class, or hit on a girl without him finding out. There was always some stoolie who saw what had happened and ran off to make a full report, exaggerating whatever it was.

For that reason, I couldn't even drink a glass of water in peace, all the more so since 80 percent of the houses around us doubled as Pentecostal revival churches. You can just imagine the piling-up of rules and prohibitions: thou shalt not masturbate; thou shalt not get it on before marriage, thou shalt not watch porn before age twenty-five; thou shalt speak either the refined French of La Bruyère or standard Lingala and never jumble the two; thou shalt not be found anywhere near the soccer stadium, even if Real Madrid is playing Barcelona; thou shalt not wear elegant clothes, and, above all else, thou shalt not strut like Papa Wemba the year he formed his band Viva La Musica.

This final commandment was the proverbial straw that broke the camel's back. Banning our entire generation from walking like Old Bokul would be like trying to ban the Americans from dropping bombs on Iraq and Afghanistan. Can you imagine all the neuroses that would cause? What made it even worse for us was that all the neighboring countries encouraged their young people to imitate Papa Wemba's gait, while we, we were denied our birthright!

Our only outlet was to get an eyeful at Camp Lifelo. It was the one part of the city where we felt truly safe. Indeed, a billboard was hung at the entrance with sayings like THE CONGO STOPS HERE, WE ARE NOT EVEN IN AFRICA, and IT WOULD TAKE A SMALL MIRACLE FOR US TO JOIN YOUR COUNTRY!

The regulars at Camp Lifelo were demobilized troops, war veterans, retired child soldiers, roving news junkies known as "street parlia-mentarians," soldiers from the Tenth Infantry, part-time bachelors, emancipated women, incubuses, and tourists disembarking from the four corners of the globe thirsty for coltan and sex. In other words, the clientele was four hundred years ahead of the rest of the country. They lived by the dictates of Article 15, enforced the Code of Hammurabi, and subjected people guilty of adultery to the infamous lemon and ngonsu treatment.

My father didn't know anybody there. And even if someone had known him, they would've had bigger fish to fry than to go blab-bing about a colt on the loose. And so it was at Camp Lifelo we learned to strut like Papa Wemba. That is, two steps forward, five steps back, three steps forward, eight steps back, fourteen steps forward, eleven steps back—a pause for two minutes and twen-ty-seven seconds—then two steps back, three steps forward, and the icing on the cake: a wild laugh, our pants cinched above the belly button, long, untucked shirts, alligator-skin shoes harvested from the Amazon, hair buzzed to within half an inch of our skulls, arms dangling slightly backward like planes coming in for a landing, necks straight, Kinshasan sangfroid and the effortless ease of Jean Sarkozy.

Upon entering Camp Lifelo, if you went straight, you ended up at a warehouse. On your left was Club DUI, where we used to get totally clobbered. We weren't the only ones. The soldiers would turn up, brandishing their bayonets and firing shots into the air as a sign of joy. The tourists, as well, materialized uninvited, reeking of gold, copper, and iron-rich bauxite, followed by young female escorts from the mines with big-tomato breasts.

A band played every night. The one and only song, "Général asi abali ngai kasi nakoki kodivorcer," lasted five hours, four of which consisted purely of sebene instrumental bridges and gyrating hips. The band leader would sing two verses and then peel off, exiting through the back door to go make love to his wife or eat fritters, or something like that. He always returned a few minutes before the end of the show. Then the crowd would roar, "Toza na système ya lifelo ve dire moto eza kopela mais tozozika te!" He would wait for the song to end, walk back up to the mike swinging his big belly, sing the same opening verses, and sneak back out all over again to go make love to his wife or scarf down fritters, or something like that.

SOLITUDE 51

I am the child of more than one mother
all the more reason not to come wring my neck or extract my teeth
    or cut off my leg or purloin my genitals, using the poor excuse I
    was born abroad at differing times . . .

SOLITUDE 88

do you ever feel like grabbing the sun and tossing it from the window until it scatters like a die, revealing fate's chosen number?

SOLITUDE 22

we won't recycle
this fetal monarch
we'll drink up his blood like djudju juice
we'll drag his corpse along the boulevard
from Kinshasa-East to Kinshasa-West
after feeding his genitals and verdant crotch
to the birds of the sky and the mountain gorillas of Kivu

SOLITUDE 20

my solitude is wider than the Indian Ocean . . .
I wonder if you can hear me scream
revelations of madness
through these walls of silence . . .

SOLITUDE 70

I have yet to scatter my body
still clattering around in my flesh
somewhere between my peduncles and right femur
fate of a warthog or migratory bird
what does the languor of rotten luck matter
don't surrender your arms until you've emptied your clip

SOLITUDE 31

my words are gutted in the gut . . .
I house my sounds in silence
my mouth aches to speak
the prophecies of the thirty-second month . . .

SOLITUDE 7

It's 1:58 PM. I live on the seventh floor. I carry my trash down-stairs. The elevators are all out of order (since '89, they tell me). I still have bottle shards embedded in my forehead. I squint from wading through clouds of cigarette smoke. I've grown thinner. I never really weighed much to begin with: ninety-seven pounds at almost six foot three. I practically swim in my pajamas. I've been vomiting nonstop since this morning. I've thrown up seven-teen beers, a salad, a dessert, if you can call it that, of cabbage and grilled potatoes . . . I feel like I'm going to cough up my belly, my guts, my innards.

I call Brigitte. Rude as ever, she tells me to go see a veterinarian. "Mwana ya makango! Sham poet moko boye! You'll end up like a stuck pig!" She repeats herself and hangs up the phone. Some women, really, are too much . . . Had she forgotten the 453 love poems I had dedicated to her last winter? And to think that every one of them began so well, "O rebellious beauty, on the bright hills, even the rebels with their lovely incisors cannot make you less lovely because you're beautiful and that's . . . indisputable."

Anyhow, she was the one who had pushed me to become a poet, threatening outright to cut off my allowance, if not report me to the police. "I want you to compose two odes to my new hairstyle," she ordered. "My blue dress is well worthy of a sonnet, don't you think? I want you to outdo Senghor. Write a series of five poems about my lips. Why don't my legs ever appear in your poetry? Don't my thighs inspire you at all? If you go downstairs one more time to play Scrabble with the Kaczorowskis, I'm going to call up the immigration service." Some women, really, are too much . . . Had she forgotten it was for her sake I'd gotten beat up and held prisoner for two days and nights in the cellar of Club Cuba, a.k.a. Club da Seleçao? Had she even managed to forget the samba incident and our tussles with Sergei, Miguel, Cheng Zhi, and Nguza, alias Old Buka Bikila? Well, you get the picture.

Anyone who has been in my tiny living room can understand my passion—even if there's no Mel Gibson around to make a movie about it. (It's pretty obvious, I think, the movies have never interested me much anyway. Mr. Gibson won't find me lining up to watch one of his videos. To be perfectly honest, I've never found anything interesting enough to pull me away from my bottles. It's pretty absurd, when you come down to it, to think that people— who are supposed to be sitting at home watching the eight o'clock news or helping their kids with their homework—instead climb all over each other to go to the movies. You have to pay for your metro ride, you have to pay for your bus ticket. If it's raining or snowing, you soak your shoes. You get there, you have to wait in line, you're bunched up against everyone else, and then you only get two hours' worth of entertainment for your money. What! You gotta be kidding, right? Between two hours at the movies and a week of drinking at Club Cuba, the choice is a no-brainer.) So, I was saying that anyone who has been inside my apartment can get a pretty good idea of my dramatic sensibility. I'm stretched out on the carpet in the form of a swastika. To my north and south, four trash bags out-stinking the toilets at Club da Seleçao. My legs are paralyzed. Pants ride halfway down my butt. I'm bare-chested. Boxers and socks in the national colors of the Republic of Zaire. Mucus and slobber flowing out my nose and mouth. I try in vain to row toward the door.

It's 6:37 PM. Playing in the background, "Teacher Don't Teach Me Nonsense," Fela Kuti. I've moved on to vomiting up the day before yesterday's matembele stew. Is there a dermatologist, or even a veterinarian, out there among you—huuuuuaaaagggggghhhhhh, blaaaaaaargh, Bri-Bri-gi-Bri-gi-Brigi-tte-Brigitteeeeeee!

SOLITUDE 77

The Congo won't slide easily into old age. The river is still beautiful, supple, raging, sultry, like a girl just ripened, with big-tomato breasts and wooded-savanna hair and thunder thighs and full lips determined to make us drool, to make our tongues wag, to go nzonzing . . . Even Diogo Cão (God rest his soul) knew that the history of this river is of a sea to drink dry, a sea to hurl against the panes of certain madcap ideas . . . The history of the river, a wound, fresh and suppurant, a filthy wound, a crushed-up vimba . . .

SOLITUDE 5

I was lucky to lose any sense of direction early on

I still believe that Zimbabwe is found in South America, that Russia

    is a peninsula, that Iraq shares a border with the Kingdom

    of Belgium, and that Italy is a province of Pakistan just as

    Palestine is the spanking new capital of Moscow

SOLITUDE 93

The fourth angel poured his bowl on the sun, and it was allowed to scorch men with fire; men were scorched by the fierce heat, and they cursed the name of God who had power over these plagues, and they did not repent and give him glory.

The fifth angel poured his bowl on the throne of the beast, and its kingdom was in darkness; men gnawed their tongues in anguish and cursed the God of heaven for their pain and sores, and did not repent of their deeds.

(Revelation 16:8–11, RSV)

SOLITUDE 54

Learn to see the world through blue-, yellow-, green- and rose-tinted glasses . . . Aim to finish everything on your plate, to drain your bottles to the last drop, to smoke your cigarettes down to the filter . . .

Make your way to the local barbershop. Brush your teeth. Draw a warm bath. Put on your best shirt. And then head down, in triumph, to Club Cuba. Salsa is a religion just like jazz and liquor of dubious proof made in Tanzania . . .

It serves no purpose to dwell all day on the legend of the country that slit its kids' throats in the dining room before dragging their bodies the length of the river. If you still can't spit out your sour luck, visit the zoo. They've got a few monkeys, a pig, three parakeets, two shipwrecked crocodiles . . .

HOLLYWOOD CITY, and in smaller letters, MPUNDA, THE HORSE DANCE. Djabir just opened a movie theater. It's not really a movie theater. Six and a half feet by ten feet, four inches, smaller than a bathroom stall at the White House. But where you can catch silent films and the latest Jackie Chan. Some say that dulls the feeling of emptiness inside . . .

SOLITUDE 97

if I had two sets of genitals, what pleasure! or rather if I had
two bodies, that is, two brains, two hearts, two sets of lungs and
    genitals, and four legs, and could thus, for example, be at one
    and the same time in Rio and Musumba, in Prague and Soweto,
    in Tangiers and Kasumbalesa . . .

SOLITUDE 60

for all the Congolese killed in Kin-la-Jungle and thrown into the river

is it my fault if the river
spits out at Brazza
the bodies thrown in at night
at Kin
in the hope of leaving no trace . . .

their favorite pastime
killing and dumping
corpse upon corpse
upended
into the arms of the river

God only knows
how many of our own
the river has eaten
then aborted
at Brazza and the Îles-de-Mbamu
since the advent of the sham

one day
to give a reckoning
the river will have to
learn to speak a new tongue
to spell the names of all the corpses

from Anita Amundala to Floribert Chebeya
without forgetting Fidèle Bazana

its complicit silence
makes me sick . . .
it's as if I had
the mbasu between my thighs

SOLITUDE 85B

I swallow my spit
since I refuse to ruin my stomach
on the crumbs dropped from your tables
forgive me if I laugh
you dare to call even that, manna
your "manna" from Sodom and Gomorrah
eat it yourself

SOLITUDE 99 *or Esperanza Club*

9:17 PM. 9:24 PM. 10:41 PM. 10:57 PM. 11:08 PM. 11:37 PM . . . Every
night began and ended the same way, or just about. The doors were
torn off. The tables flipped over. The windows broken. The bottles
of beer, lutuku, supu na tolo, tshibuku, and tropical vodka were
smashed. People danced pachanga, slugged one another, screamed
like wild beasts. People swore by every god, hollered, pulled out
their hair, hurled insults, rolled on the bare ground, even set them-
selves alight.

They wondered aloud why Podolski had curled his shot over the
crossbar, why Ballack had trapped the ball and dribbled past three
defenders instead of trapping it, dribbling once, and striking with
his left foot, why Drogba had passed to Torres instead of trying
to lob it over the keeper, why Casillas had blown it every time he
rushed off his line, why Eto'o had not given his best . . .

There was the hulk of a police station nearby. The cops spent their
days there playing cards, spouting drivel, and getting drunk on
liquor from Brazza smuggled in via Ngobila Beach. They always
waited until the brawls reached Pokou Pokou Street before lifting
a finger. Then they turned up, barefoot, tripping over themselves,
shirts open to their belly buttons, emptying their magazines into
the belly of the night . . .

The rain of bottles continued overhead. No one backed down
because everyone knew the police station, measuring thirteen

feet by thirteen feet, or sixteen feet by thirteen feet, or ten feet by twenty feet, depending who you asked—smaller, at any rate, than a bathroom stall at the White House—couldn't hold more than ten cops. And so, the clashes continued, punctuated by the crackle of gunfire. The monologue of our cherished police officers' Kalashnikovs was answered by salvos of heavy and semiautomatic fire from bored rebels who crossed the river on Saturdays and Sundays to toy with the girls from Club Marilou with big-tomato breasts, to hold up a casino, or to make illicit deliveries . . .

Revelation 17:5–12. Moaning. Born-again Christian rhapsodies. Brain-popping pollution from the cars. Dying breaths. Machine-gun warning shots.

Barking of rabid dogs. The cops holed up in their station smaller than a bathroom stall at the White House.

Mewing of feral cats. Dirty-toothed rebels . . . Vagrants lying all over the place . . . Imbroglio or demented architecture, the chaos stretching into the wee hours. No way Özil should have scored there, Messi should've never taken a dive in the penalty area, Ribéry's free kick, mamma mia! Oh Klose, ah Cannavaro, Manchester ya biso . . . Jeremiads. Sniveling. Ah, Schalke équipe ya sika . . . Cries. Hoarse shouts. The brawls spiraling from minutes to hours before petering out at the train station, having passed by Caminho de Ferro Street, Terra Nova Roundabout, Cabu Bridge, Minhas Queixas Cafe, Lycée Pilo del Baca . . .

After that, all was quiet until around eleven in the morning. Then the kids went off to school. The wounded hauled themselves to the only health clinic in the neighborhood. And everybody else— except for the five cops in the police station, the entire city was out of work—hurried south or east, to the train station or the port, searching for something to eat . . .

A gust of solitude swept across the city. A mouthless, amputee sun . . . A dirty, gray sky.

Gnarled heat, nostalgia do lagarto . . . the roads empty of human flesh . . . On Crushed Dog Boulevard, whiffs of the metallic voice of Cesária Évora from a transistor radio:

Quem mostra'bo | Ess caminho longe?
Quem mostra'bo
Ess caminho longe?
Ess caminho
Pa São Tomé
Sodade sodade sodade
Dess nha terra São Nicolau . . .

In early afternoon, the needle swung west. Everybody ran in the direction of Esperanza Club.

Men; women; former child soldiers; future child soldiers; water hawkers; gunrunners; retired fledgling journalists; dream merchants; itinerant doctors; gold diggers; listless musicians; famished students, their tongues lolling out; sex-starved prophets; fake undercover spies; school kids whose mouths stank of the Lunda

Norte railway station; adventurers of all kinds; cockroach-eaters; ex-militiamen known as "ampicillins" for their red berets and gaudy black uniforms, having fought in Angola, Rwanda, Congo–Brazzaville, Zaire, Somalia, Uganda, Afghanistan, Iraq, and Darfur, ready to throw themselves into any rebellion whatsoever provided it pays, bloodshot stoner eyes, distant gazes, voices wrecked by second-lip cigarettes . . .

Ya Zaza alias Bluebird alias The Turkey alias Sebruda alias Nzombo of the Night alias The Negro alias El Conquistador alias Old Twenty-Five alias Ethiopia alias The Full Package alias Gestapo, alias Field Marshal alias MP3 alias Four-Star General was the acknowledged owner of Esperanza Club. He was also the only one in town with a television set. A thirty-three-inch, black-and-white Philips he was said to have inherited from his great-grandfather, one Santiago Calabuig López.

Everyone knew the club's rituals by heart.

At 4 PM, American pro wrestling: John Cena, Batista, Randy Orton, Edge, Macho Man . . . At 5 PM, jazz standards preceded by Mozart and Beethoven, followed by Fela Kuti, Jimi Hendrix, and Miriam Makeba, *malaika nakupenda lalala* . . . At 6 PM, mini film club, Charlie Chaplin, Jackie Chan, Bruce Lee, and Tarzan. At 7 PM, the moment everyone had been waiting for, a match picked at random from the English Premier League, Bundesliga, Moldovan National Division, Russian Premier League, or Djibouti Premier League. In this way the same fans could root for Bayern Munich today and AC

Milan tomorrow, for Vita Club in the afternoon and for Galatasaray
or Chelsea in the evening, and so on and so forth.

Whenever a match started, everyone erupted in boisterous
song: let's go Bayern, go Podolski, go Ronaldo-do-do, go Ribéry!
Liverpool-pool-pool! Liverpool-pool-pool! Let's go CSKA Moscow,
olé, olé! Go Mazembeee, go Mazembeee . . .

What happened next was entirely predictable. As soon as the ref-
eree blew the final whistle, the chairs and tables started to fly . . .
Ya Zaza fled with his TV . . . In the distance, the muezzin launched
his fatwas against Pilar, Inés, Jacinto, and Inmaculada, drool-inducing
creatures of the night who officiated at 15b Resistenza Avenue . . .
so Book of Revelations . . . The brawls moved on to Gil Pedro
Street, headed for Cabu Bridge, were brought up short at the post
office, then flowed on toward São Vicente Chapel, La Navidad
Square, the Cabo Verde Cinema-Bar, the zoo—which, in terms of
animals, could boast these days only of a deaf, runty crocodile,
three monkeys, and two parakeets sick with avian flu . . .

On Pokou Pokou Street, the cops confronted us at last, spray-
ing us with their puking guns. The rebels in town to hump the
girls from Club Marilou returned fire, the songs traveled far into
the night, Bayern-hee-hee, Podolski-hee-hee, Beckham hee-hee,
Ronaldinhoheehee! until the sun, falling out of a tree, snapped its
left leg in two.

SOLITUDE 33

poetry (let's say) the dream is all we still have in this time of crisis . . .

SOLITUDE 35

as a man with an itch, I return to my past
as a still-frustrated man, I lurch into my future
alone, bawling in D minor, and as klutzy
as the day I came out of my mother's womb
my scrawny, charcoal body crosshatched
by cracks, once bitten, twice shy
perhaps, by mistake, I wasn't born Lazarus
to be reborn from my rind
three days into my putrefaction
perhaps . . .

SOLITUDE 49

We must be no different from the others, or we go unfed, or we're sent to howl with the dogs, or we unpin and drop our own skins out the lunchroom window. The new world demands we be the children of the same father and mother, conjoined siblings, twins to the nearest sixteenth of an inch . . . and that the rifle not be (nor have ever been) in our hands. We are stood up against the wall, legs apart, hands up. The tragedy is that this is not the movies.

SOLITUDE 65

I was hopelessly naive. I thought the Zaire River was mine, the Zaire River was my personal property, that it was my family's just like the Singer sewing machine my mother had inherited from her aunt or the LPs my father collected were . . .

I thought I could slice the river in quarters, ram it in my suitcase, stuff it inside my socks, and catch the next train for Rio de Janeiro. I thought it was a moveable feast, that I could dole it out as crumbs to my pals, or send it on a getaway to the Sahara.

My father used to accost me every evening when he got home from work: "Mwanza, come here! What are you going to do with your river after you grow up? Have you fed your river tonight? How old is that river of yours, again? Tell me, what country does your river belong to? You can't live with your river until you turn eighteen. Your river is not allowed in your bedroom. You know perfectly well you don't know how to swim and Noah won't save you if you start to drown."

Sundays were a godsend. We sat on the veranda, makossa crackling from my father's record player. He sucked down his bottles of beer, smoked his Gauloises, and told me—with the impeccable accent of a teacher of French as a foreign language—how the Zaire River dances the samba before offing itself in the ocean. He nicknamed me "Lena's Boy," claiming I was a river on the day I was born, that I was born not far from the Lena River in Russia, and that mother, in a former life, was the Lena. "The river-woman," he added, his gaze turned upward like the saints on the postcards he used to bring back from Italy.

In those days, I was dashing, rich, implacable, full of pride, and wicked like our African dictators. I made all the neighborhood kids squirm beneath my thumb. They would appear on my doorstep as early as 6 AM to pay me their respects with their breakfasts and pocket money. I made them get down on their knees and beg, and, in return, I told them stories about the Zaire River, my Russian roots, and the psychological profiles of various rivers, including the Yangtze. In spite of that, in geography class I was the most miserable of students. The teacher, an old friend of my father's, had long known of my passion for the river. Unwilling to confront my father over a dispute about some records, he decided to make me pay the price for their broken friendship.

Instead of talking about Greenland and port cities, as the geography curriculum dictated, he wasted his breath bashing my river. He would plunge into our classroom, sail straight to my desk, and look me right in the eye while saying things like "the Zaire River is a piddling stream – the Zaire River has a bellyache – the Zaire River is a dud – a river that's good for nothing – a lazy river – a phony river – a river full of holes . . ."

His words hit me like cannonballs. My tears rivaled the falls at Niagara. The other pupils, perfectly aware of the torture to which I was being subjected, snickered, whispered to one another, and took up the chorus of my executioner's insults. Which only added fuel to the fire of his oratory. He continued his fatwa against the river, my Zaire River: "an abominable pipsqueak of a river — a morosely grotesque, polluted river — an accidental river — what in hell could the Americans be up to that they still haven't paved over this river?"

It was utter humiliation. I wanted to die, to throw myself off the top of the National Television tower . . . The Zaire River meant a lot to me. It was my river, a river I had all to myself. I had faith in my river, the firmest of assurances, Cartesian certainty . . .

One afternoon the geography teacher went on for forty minutes making arbitrary comparisons among the world's rivers, and, of course, slandering the one river that was mine, which he called "a paltry river, a river with no future, a rivulet sick with syphilis and malaria, and on top of that, one of the most singularly unlucky and filthy-minded rivers in history." It was too much. That very evening, I made a full report to my parents, who took the matter seriously. The next day father accompanied me to school. The principal summoned the teacher in question. After some hard words between them, it was decided to put the matter to the entire class. The principal asked my classmates if it was true that the teacher devoted all his energy to spewing rubbish about the river. My classmates, who well knew what they risked once the principal left, being aware of the geography teacher's spiteful disposition, denied everything, adding that it was a total fabrication of mine, a complete fiction, and not the first time I'd cried wolf. As if to burnish their image with my torturer, without even being asked to, they booed me.

Two days later, the gangster, whose voice was hoarse from black-market cigarettes and liquor from Brazza smuggled in via Ngobila Beach, behind his thick glasses, with the duck-like gait of Charlie Chaplin, and dressed entirely in green, resumed his inquisition:

"If I were president of the republic, I'd donate this river to the Bolivians without a second thought. The Zaire River is a discredit to our country, a worthless river, a river teetering on the brink of suicide, a dinky river, a river for sale, a river that doesn't even know how to lick its chops, and grammatically incorrect besides!"

"You lie!" I shouted, in desperation. "You lie!"
Tears . . .
I took out my handkerchief . . .
He went on, it got worse . . .

"The Zaire River is a masquerade, and besides—if we're going to be honest about it—the river doesn't even exist. The Zaire River has never existed. The Zaire River is a utopia, a no place. Where the heck are the Americans to flush this dirty thing out of our beautiful country? I will personally go see Mobutu, and tell him, 'Your Excellency, Mr. President, with all due respect, divvy this thing up, give some to the Zambians, some to the Thais, some to our friends in France, some to our uncles in Belgium, some to the Angolans, to the Poles, to the Tanzanians . . .'"

I felt like I was going to throw up, I was dizzy . . . The pupils booed and booed . . . I stood up mechanically, picked up my schoolbag, and left. That was my first act of public disobedience. My classmates stopped laughing. The geography teacher tried to stop me by the hand.

"Where are you going, you little bastard?"

"To rejoin the river!"

SOLITUDE 44

Let 'em praise the Brahmaputra, let 'em write home about
the Yangtze, let 'em acclaim the Zambezi, they can flaunt the
Euphrates, go on about the Meuse, sing the Guadalquivir, elect the
Mississippi, and its sons-in-law, the Arkansas, the Missouri, and
the Ohio, I brandish the Congo, the only river that saps your con-
centration, the only river that fakes tuberculosis, the only river
that dances the tango and salsa and bolero and flamenco and the
cha-cha-cha, the only river that thumbs its nose at you, the only
river that eats meat, the only river that offs itself in the ocean, legs
together, arms crossed . . . I'll give you my hand to cut off, my
neck to wring, my body to castrate, if what I say isn't true. In any
case, I'm already castrated, and a sad sack like the Limpopo in its
spare hours. In any case, what do I have to fear? Forced mastur-
bation, the kiambi test, or murder disguised as drowning in the
waters of this very river?

SOLITUDE 101

I think of Tshela Mesu
my grandmother Julienne mua Mwanza's
next to last goat
I think of Tshela Mesu and weep
ah Tshela, ah homesickness!

SOLITUDE 83

I want to become a river, a meandering river without preface or
epilogue, if only to tug my soiled linens in my current, a river that
flings itself once and forever into the ocean, without siring kids
along the way . . .

SOLITUDE 18

How can I continue to boil my tea each morning, how can I continue to drag myself through beer-soaked nights, how can I continue to calmly smoke my cigarettes and sip my red wine when behind my back, far away, in certain corners of my country, the rifles recite their idiocies, the same idiocies? I am ashamed to eat and drink to fullness. I avoid filling up my belly to feel less guilty. The proof: for the last six years, I have taken my meals standing up, out of solidarity with these mothers who dine with one foot in the house, one foot out, in order to disappear into the forest at the first belch of a rifle . . .

SOLITUDE 72

you can cut my dick right off
if it means the sun will rise in my mouth

SOLITUDE 23

My first dream was to play sax. My last to become a river, the Congo or the Niger—little it matters!—and spend my days at peace, far from these wars you export and these famines that let you play at being proverbial Santa Clauses and Good Samaritans. What an act! You give with the left hand what you snatch away with the right. What an act! You give with both hands—scabby ones, besides!—and then you run to brag of your exploits as saviors of humanity and sleepwalking Santa Clauses expressly put on the face of the earth to grant us rice, soap, salt, palm oil, cassava flour, condoms, and djudju juice. What an act! You keep up the absurd and this theater of the absurd!

SOLITUDE 27

the river
dies
of solitude
sickness
stacked
on sickness . . .

I wouldn't want
that's for sure
to swap my place
for its

what a curse
to be
an ageless witness
to the effluvia of time

SOLITUDE 69

from watching you closely
I burned my eyes
which sea
must I bathe them in
to recover my sight . . .

SOLITUDE 42

River Congo
give us back the bodies
of Anita Amundala and Fidèle Bazana
they are still waiting for their burials
for eternal rest

SOLITUDE 87

only later did I understand the clefts in my fate after long years of wandering in the cane fields . . .

SOLITUDE 51

ravenous bulk-body
deprived of the good Lord
and birdsong
Australopithecus to truss up
who will lead me to the river
so I can wash away my sores

SOLITUDE 28

my teeth dance the polka
from too much chomping on my own flesh

SOLITUDE 62

I abdicate
I accept my canine fate
I let my blood
write the final letter
on the stairs of time

SOLITUDE 50

I watch my body being cast out the window
lacking solder to join myself to a few sad clouds, I see my blood
spill its ink on the cobblestones of some old Main Street . . .

SOLITUDE 78

I declare my freedom
the best way to keep my brain whole
the rest of my body, I throw out the window
like yesterday's scraps and garbage

SOLITUDE 16

the cracks in the sky splinter my sleep . . .
I spend the night counting stars
one, two, forty, seventy-two . . .
alone in front of me
a frog's fate!

SOLITUDE 90

I'm long past tired
of washing away my first sin
it's cost me seventeen years and counting
turning it over and over
in a half-empty bucket

SOLITUDE 14 *or pining for Laika*

Do you have to play basketball just because you're seven foot three? This is the story of Tshimbalanga, nicknamed Twentieth Century, the second youngest of my uncles. Growing up, Twentieth Century had to fend off our entire family and town. They used to hound him for not knowing how to cash in on his height, for refusing to take advantage of the precious manna that was his height, for not facing reality, for bringing shame on his relatives and family tree.

Long after supper, at breakfast, and even in the church pews, they nagged him about wasting his stature . . . Some family members even made comparisons between his height and the Congo River. "It's thanks to the Congo's length, you see," they would snicker, "it produces all the electricity we sell to the Brazzavillians, the Zambians, the Egyptians, not to mention the Tanzanians. But you, you still don't get it. With your height, you could also produce enough to satisfy everyone." If they weren't going on about the Congo, it was the big mining company Gécamines. "Gécamines," I remember them saying, "produces gold, diamonds, and copper, but certain unnamed individuals don't want to produce anything at all . . ."

At the time, I was living with my grandparents. They spent their days talking endlessly about politics, but as soon as uncle turned up, the conversation would change keys, from F-sharp to B-flat. They'd start name-dropping American basketball players who had fleets of cars and bought mansions at the drop of a hat . . . Grandma never said anything but headed straight for the TV, where she'd put on a tape of a basketball game. As for grandpa, he'd mutter indignantly, making oracular pronouncements such as "What solitude! Not to know how to eat by the sweat of your height . . . "

Uncle always left their house the same way he arrived, quietly . . . I would follow him out. He'd spit on the ground and light a cigarette in protest. "Why does everybody always gang up on you?" I asked him once. He gave me a grim smile. "And if I were born a Pygmy?" he snapped. "If I could do it all over again, I'd come back a Pygmy—and a Proto-Bantu to top it all!"

We would walk down Basanga Avenue and Babemba Avenue until we got to Mwanke Stadium, where the Mazembe football club used to train. When their practice was over, we retraced our steps along the same route, having the same conversation . . . He smoked while I talked.

We were bound to each other as if by a drug deal. He'd leave me the last quarter of each of his spliffs—called pot, powder, baker's yeast, cock-a-doodle-doo, or Apollo 11 because that stuff sent you on a trip, one hit and you found yourself in the Galápagos surrounded by girls with legs shaped like upside-down Coca-Cola bottles, in Bangladesh or Bangladash, or plain old Paris Clignancourt, seated in a restaurant eating your fumbwa and drinking Thermometer beer, the latter noted for both its powers as an aphrodisiac and its ability to flush out the radiator, i.e., to induce the runs—and, in return, I'd fill him in on everything that was being said behind his back. He always wanted to know every last little detail, what grandma was fretting about, what grandfather's latest declarations were, what the elders in the neighborhood were saying . . .

When I had nothing to share, he would get angry and threaten me. "If you're hiding something," he'd say, "I'll tell your mother about your pot-smoking," and since I didn't want mom to connect the dots between my uncle's height, the brain-splitting spliffs, my playing hooky with my friends, and my below-average grades, I made up or rehashed some comparison, for example, that they had said he was nearly as tall as the mango tree in the garden . . .

He would get annoyed and swear, "I'll leave, I'll show them . . ." And one fine day, he did, but not for the United States to try his luck with the Lakers or Chicago Bulls like the entire neighborhood had hoped, but for Mbuji-Mayi to come into his share of diamonds . . . It's been fourteen years since he left, fourteen years to the very day, and I miss him . . .

If he was here, I wouldn't have to spend my days worrying about him. At my grandparents' house, he kept silent or said only a few words, but during our walks he waxed eloquent and took me on vicarious trips around the globe. I can still see the gleam in his eye when he talked about Napoleon at the Battle of Waterloo. His eyes blazing as bright as the headlights on Ya Djibril's old car. He'd stop smoking. His tone suddenly solemn. He'd shake his head and speak louder. "When Leo understood he was going to lose the battle, he thought back to his childhood in Ajaccio . . ."

"Leo" was how he shortened Napoleon's name. Since he told me the same stories every day, he explained, we needed to save time. And so Napoleon became Leo; Lenin, Neli; Stalin, Tina; Hannibal, Annie, or sometimes even Nina . . .

I was very fond of all the stories that had to do with Russia. He was too. He would cry his eyes out when telling me how the Russians had launched a spacecraft into orbit with a female dog, Laika, on board. You had to have been there to appreciate the poetry that radiated from his face when he said the name "Laika." He'd close his eyes, sniff the air, take a deep breath, and burst out, "Laika! Laika!" To hear him, you would've thought he was Diogo Cão discovering the mouth of the Congo River or Archimedes, his body immersed in a liquid, pushing upward against a buoyant force equal to—so Archimedes calculated—the weight of such-and-such an amount of boiled peanuts and cassava flour.

Uncle even admitted to me that when his radiator was in need of flushing, the simple fact of murmuring "Laika, Laika" relieved his discomfort. One evening I asked him why we didn't abbreviate the name Laika like the others. He grimaced. "Can you imagine me shortening Laika's name? Laika. You don't abbreviate Laika," and then his voice trailed off, lost in a long sob . . .

I cried along with him without really knowing why the tears streamed down our faces: was it the death of Laika? The quasi-heroic death of Laika? The tragic death of Laika? The Russian genius to send a poor brute of an animal into space? The Russian genius to send an animal one might keep as a pet into space? Each

time we wiped away our tears, I asked him, "Why are we crying?"
He'd stammer in reply, "It's too much. Too much. Ohhh, Laika.
Ohhh, Laika," and immediately upon those words, both of us
would start bawling again.

Around that time, we ran into one of his friends, Ya Nicky, on
our way home. "I'm off to sign up at Old Kabwe's," Ya Nicky
told us. "Come with me, and we'll walk together." The Old Kabwe
in question was hardly twenty-six years old. They called him
old because of his hair, which was already white, and most of
all because of his broad experience. He was what's known as a
"collectionneur." According to the *Larousse Pocket Dictionary*
(which, its name notwithstanding, can very well be carried in a
backpack), according to the *Petit Robert Dictionary*, not to men-
tion the testimony of little Robert's uncle and younger brother, a
collectionneur is a person who gathers dogmeat to sell it at retail
or discount prices.

Old Kabwe operated a small restaurant and butcher shop. And
since 80 percent of the young people in the neighborhood were
crazy about dog stews, you had to sign up four or even five
weeks in advance to have a prayer of being served. Dog omelet,
stuffed dog breast, dog schnitzel on a bed of cassava leaves, dog
cutlets à la moutarde, sautéed puppy, braised bulldog in pili-pili
sauce, and so on. When we got there, Ya Nicky signed up and—
if you could believe it—found himself all the way down at num-
ber one hundred and eighteen on the list. "Since we've known
each other since we were kids," Old Kabwe said reassuringly, "I'll
bump you up to eighty-eight." Before we left, my uncle also made

arrangements for a dog, not for eating, but to keep as his pet. Old Kabwe and Ya Nicky burst out laughing . . .

(Open parenthesis. At the time, rumors circulated throughout the neighborhood to the effect that puppy kebabs with crayfish served three functions: to extend any sort of sexual activity by forty minutes, to facilitate insomnia, and finally to bulk up one's midsection. And thus, since I wanted to gain weight, sleep less, and last longer, I went to eat my kebabs at Old Kabwe's. My dream was to have a big belly, three or four wives, and seventeen children—eight girls and nine boys—and to walk stooped over as if I had a permanent case of dysentery. Close parenthesis.)

After six months of saving, my uncle and I went to pick up a tiny dog, just as cute as could be. Uncle started spending every afternoon behind the house playing with his puppy under the inquisitorial eye of grandfather, who would mutter under his breath, "Instead of thinking about his career, here he is fooling around with Acute Hemorrhoids!"

You see, on the night we brought his adopted dog home, my uncle declared, in a voice choked with emotion, "My dog will be called Laika." The tears streamed down both our cheeks. But no sooner than the following day someone in the family rebaptized the dog "Acute Hemorrhoids." From then on, the whole family and the entire neighborhood insisted upon calling Laika Acute Hemorrhoids. Vox populi, vox dei, as the saying goes. Poor Laika, who didn't understand the situation, began to balk at being called Laika. "Laika, Laika," you'd say. And she'd sulk, she'd whimper, she'd flat out refuse to come. But as soon as you said, "*Hem*orrhoids, Acute Hemorrhoids," she ran toward you, jumping and yipping with joy.

It was, I think, Laika's death, or Acute Hemorrhoids', depending on your preference, which convinced my uncle to leave the family for good. The day before he left, he asked me, "Are you coming with me?" I said, "Where?" He answered, "To Mbuji-Mayi." I replied, "Let me think about it." He sighed, and for the umpteenth time told me the stories about the crumbling of the walls of Jericho, the deeds of Leo, the mind games of Tina and Neli and, last but not least, the saga of Laika, employing the same tone and sequence as ever: "Laika, Laika, Russian dog and first living being to be launched into orbit aboard the spacecraft Sputnik 2, on November 3, 1957, upon the orders of Nikita Sergeyevich Khrushchev, First Secretary of the Communist Party of the Soviet Union, the pride of animal-scientists everywhere, a forerunner of our yearnings to fathom the invisible frontiers, Laika, Laika . . ."

the sun snapped its left arm
falling from a solid black sky
free fall or excessive solitude?
it depends who you ask . . .

SOLITUDE 59

Europe does not belong to me
even at my loopiest
I don't cross the red line
and mistake the old continent
for my grandparents' porch
but as far as I know of the matter
unless I am very much mistaken
unless I've had one glass too many
unless my memory doesn't serve
Europe doesn't belong to you, either!

Mister Know-it-all
splash a little water in your cheap wine
instead of wagging your tongue and yapping about exile
as if you knew its ins and outs!

the only exile you've known
is crossing the street to your maternal aunts'
and what's more, a narrow street, one hundred feet by six feet
so then, Mister Know-it-all
stop stuffing us with these choice morsels
plucked from the ramblings of your lily-livered mind . . .

Europe does not belong to you
despite the fact you began your days here—in the middle of the night,
   besides!

Mister Genius-a-bigger-genius-than-Albert-Einstein

Mister Genius-a-bigger-genius-than-Leonardo-da-Vinci

Mister Genius-a-bigger-genius-than-Johannes-Gutenberg

splash a little milk in your watered-down wine

while I listen to your half-baked theories

the train to Liège-Guillemins awaits me . . .

3:40 PM

the train to Seville awaits me . . .

4:45 PM

the train to Budapest awaits me . . .

5:56 PM

the train to Innsbruck . . .

7:00 PM

the train to . . .

SOLITUDE 15

the wind bawls itself sick
in this subway-tile sky
letting go, I vomit up my seed

SOLITUDE 94

as the river offs itself in the ocean
I go off to spill my guts

SOLITUDE 55

I see your sparkling eyes again
like the dying flames
of a fire
I try to speak to you about the Congo River . . .
at its mouth in Moanda . . .
I try to sketch the Missouri for you
pitching itself into the Mississippi . . .
I try to revive for you
the concerto-cries of these migrating birds
as they swoop through depths of sky . . .
I try to tell you the Sahel's true name
I try to trace your unspoiled face with my fingers
I try, I try, I try . . .
but you are not here . . .

SOLITUDE 84B

bolingo ya masuwa na ebale
I am lovestruck, in love with the lightning strike
await the solar eclipse
to seduce my lover with cakes
Russian cigarettes, salt, and liquor from Brazza

SOLITUDE 68

the vegetation is depression
nervousness dressed as sap bungs up
the southern hemisphere of my crucifixion
already earthworms
plan a banquet in the pit of my mouth

SOLITUDE 26

And he said to me, "The waters that you saw, where the harlot is seated, are peoples and multitudes and nations and tongues. And the ten horns that you saw, they and the beast will hate the harlot; they will make her desolate and naked, and devour her flesh and burn her up with fire."

(Revelation 17:15–16, RSV)

SOLITUDE 30

And if I ate my own penis
would you still accuse me of cannibalism?
even though it's mine?

SOLITUDE 1

licopa na ye eza léger
soki afingi tofingi
soki atie libaya, totie libaya
momeli diamba
collabo moko boye

Pilate can bellow all he wants
he can wash his hands forever
he can spend the next ten years
scrubbing his slender fingers
that won't absolve him
of his pangolin-like cowardice

we'll go down to see him
with a water cask or the entire Congo River in tow
to make sure he's got what he needs to wash with
not that that will change one whit
the depth of his betrayal

SOLITUDE 102

if I may say two words
River Congo, I won't drink your water
as long as you keep the secret
as long as you don't
spit out the bodies of my loved ones
at Brazza and Mbamu

SOLITUDE 48

in profile, my head is shaped like Africa; if you watch closely,
you'll see the Congo River flow out my windows and back into my
mouth . . .

SOLITUDE 74

I can't decide between hitting the club or taking to bed to kick out the flies, mosquitoes, and chameleons dreaming of terrae incognitae.

SOLITUDE 58

I'll vomit without further ado
better an empty stomach
than a belly full of plague

SOLITUDE 37

I still have one foot out the door, the other within

SOLITUDE 10

there, where the river runs not

they have learned to dig

they dig nights

they dig days

they bury

they bury

they bury

they bury

they bury

they bury

they bury

they bury

they bury

their rituals marked

by red wine

and dance steps

in honor

of a claustrophilic god

who throws them crumbs

from the ramparts of his capital

ordering them

to start their labors

anew

to multiply the holes

to bury

again, again, again . . .

SOLITUDE 75

I don't care for pagan holidays
they'll raise their cups without me
I won't go dance their salsa
or their polka
with its slowed-down beat
and sudden leaps from pillar to post

SOLITUDE 92

I lie down
in drunkenness
I'm not lonely
I just wish
to electrify
my life

SOLITUDE 80 = *Solitude 11* + *Solitude 17* + *Solitude 21*

asleep but not

my sun running on fumes

my skeleton unboned

and my teeth serrated

(like cassava leaves)

must I shame my own flesh

or graze my own pubes?

and yes, amen! my poetic word

is not the Gospel of John

nor the First Epistle of Paul to the Corinthians

not even the Book of Habakkuk

which is my way of telling you

I water my dreams with sleep

since my sterile, desiccated bones

derail the train to the abyss

and yes, but no, my australopithecine gullet

and yes, but neither, my protozoan mug

and yes, but no, my skeletal body

and yes, but neither, my amphibian belly

am I a toad?

the toaderino (?)

SOLITUDE 89

and you expect me
to play the tam-tam
with wrists
you just cuffed
forgive me if I laugh
are we at the circus
on the flying trapeze
or are you pumping
my stomach
forgive me if I laugh

SOLITUDE 95

I auction off my teeth and left kidney to whoever is kindest
I donate my pants with both legs still inside . . .

SOLITUDE 76

I am as old as my grandfather
if I add 45, 55, or 57 years . . .

SOLITUDE 75B

I'm going to bury myself
or rather make my burial plans
or rather wash my mortal remains
or rather place flowers and a jug of water
on my grave . . .

SOLITUDE 24

I have one foot in hell

SOLITUDE 82

the city drifts off with my debt
and my thirst to swindle the sun
quickly, saltily fizzles
must I beg the dead ground
to stoop to ease my sorrow?
a year, one whole year without
nightfall, a year of utter madness!

SOLITUDE 56

I eat, I eat, I eat
but do not feel full (*repeat*)
must I eat myself?
eat my cock and my belly?
practice cannibalism or self-cannibalism?
the main thing, to stave off
my Somalia-like famine

SOLITUDE 87C

I swallow my spit
since I refuse to feed
on the crumbs that fall from your tables—
lest eucalyptus and mango trees
invade my belly

NOTES

J. Bret Maney

SOLITUDE 71

(?): a guide to the poem's intonation. According to the poet, when a question mark is enclosed in parentheses, the reader can declaim the corresponding line as either a question or declaration.

sister Abigail: a reference to David's sister in the Hebrew Bible (1 Chronicles 2:16–17).

SOLITUDE 52

Katako-Kombe: birthplace of Patrice Émery Lumumba (1925–1961), independence leader and first prime minister of the independent Democratic Republic of Congo (DRC).

SOLITUDE 64

nzete ya mbila bazokata ezokola: "the palm tree you cut down keeps on growing." A Lingala proverb that can be used to express one's resilience in the face of an adversary.

SOLITUDE 57

oder die Poesie der Verzweiflung: "or the poetry of despair" (German).

kipelekese: dizziness, loss of memory or control after an emotional shock (Lingala).

tchanga madesu: unhealthy rations fed to army recruits during the period Laurent-Désiré Kabila was in power (1997–2001). The Katanga Swahili term is derived from "nsaka madesu," the Lingala name of a stew made of beans and cassava leaves, and the Katanga Swahili verb *kutchanga*, meaning "to mix."

ebale ezanga mokuwa: supple, free-flowing river (lit. "the river has no bones"), an expression in Lingala.

SOLITUDE 79

bapumbafu: idiots, stupid persons (Swahili).

souanpantes: a wannabe (Lingala).

bambendre: gullible fools (Lingala).

SOLITUDE 8

bibukuta-bukuta, bangubu lokoso, basemba-bilokota: "those who want their bread buttered on both sides, greedy hippos, bin divers" (Lingala).

SOLITUDE 81

Old Bokul: a nickname of the iconic Congolese rumba musician Papa Wemba (1949–2016). "Bokul" is an abbreviation of "bokulaka," which means elder, man of importance, in Lingala.

Lifelo: hell (Lingala).

Article 15: a Congolese joke about the weakness of the state, according to which an imaginary Article 15 ("l'article quinze") of the constitution instructs citizens to "fend for yourselves."

Général asi abali ngai kasi nakoki kodivorcer: the song's title can be translated as "The General has already married me but nothing stops me from getting a divorce" (Lingala).

toza na système ya lifelo ve dire moto eza kopela mais tozozika te: "We are in hell, which means the fire is raging but we don't get burned" (Lingala). From the song "Wake Up" (1996) by Congolese soukous singer Koffi Olomide (b. 1956).

SOLITUDE 22

this fetal monarch: a reference to the imposition of Joseph Kabila (b. 1971) as president of the DRC, at age twenty-nine, after his father, Laurent-Désiré Kabila, was assassinated in 2001.

SOLITUDE 7

Mwana ya makango: lout, bastard (Lingala).
sham poet moko boye!: "you sham poet!" (Lingala).

SOLITUDE 77

nzonzing: also *zonzing* (Lingala). In the music world, it refers to the practice of booking musicians outside one's group for performances. A side gig.

Diogo Cão: Portuguese captain credited with being the first European to sail into the mouth of the Congo River during the late fifteenth century. He erected a stone pillar, still standing today, claiming the area for the Portuguese king.

vimba: A yellowish flour used for pig feed that the human population in Lubumbashi, in southeastern DRC, was forced to consume during food shortages in the 1990s. In Swahili, *kuvimba* means "to swell or to fatten."

SOLITUDE 60

Kin-la-Jungle: a riff on Kinshasa's longstanding nickname "Kin-la-Belle" (lit. Kin-the-Beautiful).

Brazza: short for Brazzaville, the capital and largest city of the Republic of Congo. Brazza is located on the northern bank of the Congo River opposite Kinshasa. The Republic of Congo is also sometimes referred to as Congo–Brazzaville.

Îles-de-Mbamu: large island in the middle of the Congo River, at its widest point, just east of the capital cities of Kinshasa and Brazzaville. The poet uses the plural "îles" to denote the island proper and the many islets surrounding it.

Floribert Chebeya: executive director of the Congolese human rights organization Voice of the Voiceless, murdered after a 2010 meeting at police headquarters in Kinshasa.

Fidèle Bazana: Floribert Chebeya's driver and a member of Voice of the Voiceless, Bazana was abducted at the same time as Chebeya. His body has never been recovered. The third person cited, Anita Amundala, is an invention of the author.

mbasu: a disease characterized by intense swelling, usually of the legs. Its cause may be of mystical origin.

SOLITUDE 99

lutuku, supu na tolo, tshibuku: inexpensive, unauthorized alcohols produced locally in the DRC. Lutuku is Congolese moonshine. Tshibuku is a beer brewed from corn. Supu na tolo is a liquor of varying proof reputed to be an aphrodisiac.

Ngobila Beach: the main port of entry into Kinshasa for passengers and goods crossing the Congo River from Brazzaville.

Manchester ya biso: "our Manchester" (Lingala). A reference to the English professional soccer team Manchester United.

Schalke équipe ya sika: "Schalke, the team of the moment" (Lingala). A reference to the German professional soccer team F.C. Schalke 04.

Quem mostra'bo . . . terra São Nicolau: Who showed you / That long way? / Who showed you / That long way? / That way / To São Tomé / Saudade saudade saudade / From my homeland São Nicolau.

SOLITUDE 84B

bolingo ya masuwa na ebale: "love between boat and river" (Lingala).

SOLITUDE I

licopa na ye eza léger / soki afingi tofingi / soki atie libaya, totie libaya / momeli diamba / collabo moko boye: "his scams are fluff pieces / if he mocks us, we insult him until our mouths run dry / if he puffs out his chest, we puff out our chests / pothead / who squeals every chance he gets" (Lingala).

pangolin: a scaly, small mammal that rolls itself into a ball when under threat from predators.

TRANSLATOR'S ACKNOWLEDGMENTS

Acknowledgments are due to the editors of *Asymptote*, where some of the poems in this book first appeared. I am grateful to my editor David Shook, to Will Evans and the entire team at Deep Vellum. Thanks also to the following people for their support or assistance during the time I worked on this project: Allison Amend, Joaquim Arena, Roland Glasser, Sara Mortoni, Olivia Loksing Moy, Cristina Pérez Jiménez, Bienvenu Sene Mongaba, Christian Thanhäuser, and not least Fiston Mwanza Mujila, the *mwanza-nkongolo*, for entrusting me with his poetry.

PARTNERS

pixel ||| texel

EMBREY FAMILY
FOUNDATION

ALLRED
CAPITAL MANAGEMENT
of
RAYMOND JAMES®

ADDITIONAL DONORS, CONT'D

Mark Haber	Scott & Katy Nimmons
Mary Cline	Sherry Perry
Maynard Thomson	Sydneyann Binion
Michael Reklis	Stephen Harding
Mike Soto	Stephen Williamson
Mokhtar Ramadan	Susan Carp
Nikki & Dennis Gibson	Susan Ernst
Patrick Kukucka	Theater Jones
Patrick Kutcher	Tim Perttula
Rev. Elizabeth & Neil Moseley	Tony Thomson
Richard Meyer	

SUBSCRIBERS

Ned Russin	Erin Kubatzky
Michael Binkley	Shelby Vincent
Michael Schneiderman	Margaret Terwey
Aviya Kushner	Ben Fountain
Kenneth McClain	Caroline West
Eugenie Cha	Ryan Todd
Lance Salins	Gina Rios
Stephen Fuller	Caitlin Jans
Joseph Rebella	Ian Robinson
Brian Matthew Kim	Elena Rush
Andreea Pritcher	Courtney Sheedy
Anthony Brown	Matthew Eatough
Michael Lighty	Elif Ağanoğlu
Kasia Bartoszynska	

AVAILABLE NOW FROM DEEP VELLUM

MICHÈLE AUDIN · *One Hundred Twenty-One Days*
translated by Christiana Hills · FRANCE

BAE SUAH · *Recitation*
translated by Deborah Smith · SOUTH KOREA

MARIO BELLATIN · *Mrs. Murakami's Garden*
translated by Heather Cleary · MEXICO

EDUARDO BERTI · *The Imagined Land*
translated by Charlotte Coombe · ARGENTINA

CARMEN BOULLOSA · *Texas: The Great Theft* · *Before* · *Heavens on Earth*
translated by Samantha Schnee · Peter Bush · Shelby Vincent · MEXICO

MAGDA CARNECI · *FEM*
translated by Sean Cotter · ROMANIA

MATHILDE CLARK · *Lone Star*
translated by Martin Aitken · DENMARK

LEILA S. CHUDORI · *Home*
translated by John H. McGlynn · INDONESIA

SARAH CLEAVE, ed. · *Banthology: Stories from Banned Nations* ·
IRAN, IRAQ, LIBYA, SOMALIA, SUDAN, SYRIA & YEMEN

ANANDA DEVI · *Eve Out of Her Ruins*
translated by Jeffrey Zuckerman · MAURITIUS

PETER DIMOCK · *Daybook from Sheep Meadow* · USA

CLAUDIA ULLOA DONOSO · *Little Bird*, translated by Lily Meyer · PERU/NORWAY

ROSS FARRAR · *Ross Sings Cheree & the Animated Dark: Poems* · USA

ALISA GANIEVA · *Bride and Groom* · *The Mountain and the Wall*
translated by Carol Apollonio · RUSSIA

ANNE GARRÉTA · *Sphinx* · *Not One Day* · *In Concrete*
translated by Emma Ramadan · FRANCE

JÓN GNARR · *The Indian* · *The Pirate* · *The Outlaw*
translated by Lytton Smith · ICELAND

GOETHE · *The Golden Goblet: Selected Poems* · *Faust, Part One*
translated by Zsuzsanna Ozsváth and Frederick Turner · GERMANY

NOEMI JAFFE · *What are the Blind Men Dreaming?*
translated by Julia Sanches & Ellen Elias-Bursac · BRAZIL

CLAUDIA SALAZAR JIMÉNEZ · *Blood of the Dawn*
translated by Elizabeth Bryer · PERU

JUNG YOUNG MOON · *Seven Samurai Swept Away in a River* · *Vaseline Buddha*
translated by Yewon Jung · SOUTH KOREA

KIM YIDEUM · *Blood Sisters*
translated by Ji yoon Lee · SOUTH KOREA

JOSEFINE KLOUGART · *Of Darkness*
translated by Martin Aitken · DENMARK

YANICK LAHENS · *Moonbath*
translated by Emily Gogolak · HAITI

FORTHCOMING FROM DEEP VELLUM

SHANE ANDERSON • *After the Oracle* • USA

MARIO BELLATIN • *Beauty Salon* • translated by David Shook • MEXICO

MIRCEA CĂRTĂRESCU · *Solenoid*
translated by Sean Cotter · ROMANIA

LOGEN CURE · *Welcome to Midland: Poems* · USA

LEYLÂ ERBIL · *A Strange Woman*
translated by Nermin Menemencioğlu · TURKEY

RADNA FABIAS • *Habitus* • translated by David Colmer • NETHERLANDS

SARA GOUDARZI • *The Almond in the Apricot* • USA

SONG LIN • *The Gleaner Song* • translated by Dong Li • CHINA

JUNG YOUNG MOON · *Arriving in a Thick Fog*
translated by Mah Eunji and Jeffrey Karvonen · SOUTH KOREA

FISTON MWANZA MUJILA · *The Villain's Dance*, translated by Roland Glasser
DEMOCRATIC REPUBLIC OF CONGO

JOHNATHAN NORTON • *Penny Candy* • USA

LUDMILLA PETRUSHEVSKAYA · *Kidnapped: A Crime Story*, translated by Marian
Schwartz · *The New Adventures of Helen: Magical Tales*, translated by Jane Bugaeva ·
RUSSIA

SERGIO PITOL • *The Love Parade* • translated by G. B. Henson • MEXICO

MANON STEFAN ROS · *The Blue Book of Nebo* · WALES

ETHAN RUTHERFORD · *Farthest South & Other Stories* · USA

BOB TRAMMELL · *The Origins of the Avant-Garde in Dallas & Other Stories* · USA